# Little Chefs Cooking In The Kitchen

"Little Chefs Cooking In The Kitchen" is a delightful and educational introduction to the world of cooking for children. This engaging and interactive experience aims to ignite a passion for culinary exploration in young minds, fostering creativity, teamwork, and a love for wholesome food.

## Setting the Scene:

**Enchanting Kitchen Environment:** The kitchen is transformed into a magical realm where young chefs embark on exciting culinary adventures. Child-sized aprons, colorful utensils, and chef hats create an inviting atmosphere, encouraging a sense of ownership and excitement.

## Objectives:

1. **Educational Exploration:** Little Chefs Cooking introduces children to the basics of cooking through a hands-on and age-appropriate approach. They learn about various ingredients, kitchen tools, and the art of combining flavors.
2. **Creativity and Imagination:** The program encourages creativity by allowing little chefs to experiment with different ingredients, colors, and textures. Through this, they not only develop

cooking skills but also enhance their imaginative thinking.

3. **Teamwork and Social Skills:** Working in a shared kitchen space fosters a sense of camaraderie among the little chefs. They learn the importance of teamwork, communication, and sharing responsibilities to create a delicious masterpiece.

## Activities:

1. **Simple Recipe Creations:** The program includes easy and safe recipes tailored to the age group, such as making colorful fruit salads, assembling sandwiches, or decorating cupcakes. Each recipe is designed to be achievable for little hands with minimal adult assistance.
2. **Ingredient Exploration:** Little chefs get hands-on experience with different ingredients, learning about their origins, flavors, and nutritional benefits. This adds an educational element to the cooking adventure.
3. **Storytelling Sessions:** Interspersed with cooking activities are storytelling sessions that revolve around food, fostering a connection between literature and culinary experiences. This not only enhances language skills but also deepens their appreciation for the storytelling aspect of cooking.

## Safety Measures:

1. **Supervised Environment:** Trained instructors or parents supervise the kitchen activities, ensuring a safe and controlled environment for the little chefs.
2. **Age-Appropriate Tools:** The kitchen is equipped with child-friendly, safe tools and utensils designed for their small hands, promoting independence and confidence.

## Conclusion:

"Little Chefs Cooking in a Kitchen" is a delightful journey where children not only learn the art of cooking but also develop essential life skills in a fun and interactive way. Through this imaginative and educational experience, young chefs are empowered to explore the world of flavors, fostering a lifelong love for good food and the joy of cooking.

**Let's start with proper handwashing in the kitchen**

Proper handwashing is a crucial aspect of kitchen hygiene. Here's a simplified guide for little chefs:

# Little Chef's Guide to Proper Handwashing in the Kitchen:

1. **Gather Supplies:**

   - Soap (fun and colorful if possible!)
   - A small step stool if needed

2. **Step up to the Sink:**

   - Stand on the step stool if necessary to reach the sink comfortably.

3. **Turn on the Water:**

   - Use warm water; not too hot and not too cold.

4. **Wet Your Hands:**

   - Wet your hands thoroughly under the running water.

5. **Soap Up:**

   - Grab some soap (make sure it's enough to create bubbles!) and rub your hands together. Don't forget between your fingers and under your nails.

6. **Sing a Song:**

- Sing your favorite song (like the "Happy Birthday" song) while scrubbing. This makes sure you're washing for at least 20 seconds.

7. **Rinse:**

- Rinse off the soap under the running water. Wiggle your fingers to get all the soap off.

8. **Dry Off:**

- Use a clean towel to dry your hands. If you don't have a towel, you can air-dry them.

9. **Done!**

- You're now a handwashing pro! Clean hands are ready for cooking fun.

**Remember:**

- Wash your hands before and after handling food, especially if you've been touching anything dirty.
- If your hands get dirty while cooking, it's okay to stop and wash them before continuing.

## Why is Handwashing Important?

- Keeps germs away, so the food stays clean and safe to eat.
- It's a good habit for staying healthy and happy!

# Tip for Grown-Ups:

- Supervise the handwashing process until the little chef gets the hang of it.

Teaching kids the importance of handwashing in the kitchen not only ensures their safety but also lays the foundation for good hygiene habits that will stay with them as they continue to explore the world of cooking.

**Remember the food danger zone, what it is and why it is important;**

**Let's simplify the concept of the "Food Danger Zone" for little chefs:**

# The Food Danger Zone - What and Why:

### What is the Food Danger Zone?

The Food Danger Zone is a temperature range where harmful bacteria love to grow on food. It's between **40°F (4°C) and 140°F (60°C)**.

### Why is it Important?

1. **Bacteria Party:** Between these temperatures, bacteria multiply super fast, like having a big party. We don't want that!

2. **Keep Food Safe:** If food stays in this danger zone for too long, it can make us sick when we eat it. Yucky!

**How to Stay Safe:**

- **Keep it Cool:** Store cold food in the fridge at or below 40°F (4°C).
- **Keep it Hot:** Keep hot food hot, above 140°F (60°C).
- **Don't Linger:** Don't let food hang out in the danger zone. Cook it, eat it, or chill it!

**Remember:**

- **Cold and Hot are A-OK:** Food is safe when it's really cold or really hot. In between, not so much.

**Why Grown-Ups Care:**

- Grown-ups want to make sure the food we eat is yummy and won't make us sick. Following the rules about the Food Danger Zone helps keep everyone healthy and happy!

Teaching little chefs about the Food Danger Zone in simple terms helps them understand why it's important to handle and store food properly to keep it safe and delicious!

**How to properly take the temperature of food?**

Taking the temperature of food is like checking if it's wearing the right "doneness" outfit. Here's a simplified guide for little chefs:

## Little Chef's Guide to Checking Food Temperature:

**What You Need:**

- A food thermometer (it's like a magic wand for food).

**How to Do It:**

1. **Wash Your Hands:**
   - Always start with clean hands. A quick handwash, just like before cooking!
2. **Get Your Thermometer Ready:**
   - If your food thermometer has a pointy end, be careful! It's not a toy.
3. **Stick It In:**
   - Gently stick the thermometer into the thickest part of the food. For example, if you're checking chicken, aim for the middle part.
4. **Wait a Little:**

- The thermometer needs a moment to do its magic. Be patient, and don't wiggle it around.

5. **Read the Number:**
   - Look at the number on the thermometer. That's the temperature of your food!

6. **Check the Chart:**
   - Know the magic numbers for different foods. For example, chicken should be at least 165°F (74°C).

7. **Done or Not?**
   - If the number is right, your food is ready to party! If not, keep cooking until it is.

**Why It's Cool:**

- Checking the temperature makes sure our food is cooked perfectly. It's like giving it a high-five for being safe and yummy!

**Tip for Grown-Ups:**

- Help the little chef with the thermometer until they get the hang of it. It's a teamwork magic trick!

Learning to use a food thermometer is a superpower that helps little chefs make sure their meals are not just tasty but also safe to eat. It's like having a temperature superhero in the kitchen!

**How to properly use a knife and peeling vegetables correctly?**

Absolutely, using a knife and peeling vegetables can be a fun and safe kitchen adventure for little chefs. Here's a simplified guide:

## Little Chef's Guide to Using a Knife and Peeling Vegetables:

**1. Get the Right Tools:**

- Choose a kid-friendly knife (with adult supervision) and a vegetable peeler. Make sure they are sharp but not too sharp.

**2. Wash Your Hands:**

- Just like superheroes, clean hands are ready for action!

**3. Knife Time:**

- Hold the knife with one hand and the food with the other.
- **Keep Fingers Safe:** Tuck your fingers in, so they're like a little fort protecting you from the knife.

## 4. Slice, Don't Dice:

- Practice slicing motions first. Slow and steady wins the slicing race.

## 5. Rolling Chop:

- For round veggies like carrots, use a rolling chop. Roll the veggie away from you and chop as it rolls.

## 6. Peeling Magic:

- Hold the vegetable in one hand and the peeler in the other.
- **Away, Not Toward:** Peel away from your fingers, not toward. Safety first!

## 7. Potato Rule:

- For potatoes, cut them in half, so they don't roll around. It's like giving them a little nap before getting peeled.

## 8. Watch Those Knuckles:

- Keep your knuckles safe by curling them in when using the knife. Knuckles are like superheroes protecting your fingers!

## 9. Super Important:

- Always have a grown-up nearby when using knives. They're the kitchen superheroes!

**Why It's Awesome:**

- Using a knife and peeler turns veggies into cool shapes. Plus, it's like being a kitchen artist!

**Tip for Grown-Ups:**

- Teach and supervise until the little chef becomes a vegetable-cutting maestro.

Learning to handle knives and peelers is a step towards becoming a kitchen superhero. With the right skills, little chefs can transform veggies into tasty creations while staying safe and having fun!

## What are all the utensils most important for a Little Chef?

Creating a safe and enjoyable cooking experience for a Little Chef involves having a set of kid-friendly utensils. Here's a list of essential utensils for little chefs:

# 1. Mixing Bowls:

- Perfect for stirring, mixing, and creating magic in the kitchen.

## 2. Measuring Cups and Spoons:

- Teaches little chefs about quantities while keeping the mess to a minimum.

## 3. Kid-Friendly Knife:

- A safe, age-appropriate knife for chopping and slicing under adult supervision.

## 4. Vegetable Peeler:

- Makes peeling fruits and veggies a breeze.

## 5. Wooden Spoon:

- Great for stirring, mixing, and not scratching pots and pans.

## 6. Spatula:

- Perfect for flipping pancakes or cookies with ease.

## 7. Whisk:

- Whipping up eggs or creating smooth batters becomes a fun task.

## 8. Rolling Pin:

- Essential for rolling out dough for cookies or pies.

## 9. Cutting Board:

- Provides a safe surface for cutting and chopping.

## 10. Fun Apron:

- Sets the stage for a little chef's culinary adventures and keeps clothes clean.

## 11. Mixing Spoon:

- Long-handled and sturdy for mixing ingredients in big bowls.

## 12. Decorating Tools:

- Sprinkles, piping bags, and cookie cutters for adding creative touches.

## 13. Baking Sheets and Pans:

- Sized appropriately for little hands, for baking cookies, muffins, and more.

## 14. Tongs:

- Ideal for grabbing and flipping items while cooking.

## 15. Colander:

- For washing fruits and veggies or draining pasta.

## 16. Child-Safe Peeler:

- A peeler designed for little hands to help with fruit and vegetable prep.

## 17. Fun Plates and Bowls:

- Make mealtime more exciting with colorful and interesting plates and bowls.

## 18. Timer:

- An easy-to-use timer for little chefs to keep track of cooking times.

## 19. Pastry Brush:

- Perfect for brushing on egg wash or melted butter.

## 20. Muffin Tin:

- Ideal for making mini muffins or cupcakes.

## 21. Fun Cookie Sheets:

- Non-stick, kid-sized cookie sheets for baking adventures.

## 22. Safety Step Stool:

- Helps little chefs reach the countertop comfortably and safely.

## 23. Silicone Utensils:

- Non-scratch and safe for use with different cookware.

## 24. Ladle:

- Makes serving soups and stews a manageable task.

## 25. Plastic or Wooden Utensils:

- Utensils that won't scratch or damage cookware.

Having a set of kid-friendly utensils not only makes cooking safe but also adds an element of excitement to the kitchen, encouraging a love for food and cooking from an early age.

How do you correctly measure dry and wet ingredients?

Measuring dry and wet ingredients is like following a recipe treasure map. Here's a simplified guide for little chefs:

## Measuring Dry Ingredients:

**What You Need:**

- Dry ingredient (like flour, sugar, or rice)
- Measuring cups

**How to Do It:**

1. **Scoop it Up:**
   - Use a spoon to gently scoop the dry ingredient into the measuring cup.
2. **Level it Off:**
   - Take the back of a knife or a flat spatula and level off the ingredient so it's flat on top.
3. **Ready to Pour:**
   - Pour it into your mixing bowl or container. Your dry ingredient is all set!

**Why It's Cool:**

- This makes sure you have just the right amount for your recipe. No extra, no less!

## Measuring Wet Ingredients:

**What You Need:**

- Wet ingredient (like milk, oil, or water)
- Measuring cups (the ones specifically for liquids)

**How to Do It:**

1. **Pour it In:**
   - Fill the measuring cup to the brim with the wet ingredient.
2. **Check at Eye Level:**
   - Bend down to eye level and make sure the liquid is right at the line. It's like checking a mini swimming pool!
3. **Ready to Mix:**
   - Pour it into your mixing bowl. Your wet ingredient is good to go!

**Why It's Cool:**

- Just like dry ingredients, measuring liquids ensures your recipe turns out just the way it's supposed to be—yummy!

## Extra Tips:

- **Teamwork Time:** If you have a grown-up helper, they can hold the measuring cup while you pour.
- **Have Fun:** Pretend you're a chef on a cooking show, and measure with style!
- **Be Patient:** Take your time, and remember, measuring is like a little kitchen adventure.

## Remember:

- Dry ingredients stay put in the cup, while wet ingredients like to flow. Each needs its special measuring cup.

Learning to measure is like being a kitchen scientist. Follow the recipe, measure carefully, and voilà — you've unlocked the magic of cooking!

**Let's start with simple snacks that little chefs can make:**

Here are some simple and fun snack ideas that little chefs can make with minimal assistance:

## 1. Fruit Kabobs:

Ingredients:

- Assorted fruits (grapes, strawberries, melon chunks)
- Wooden skewers

Steps:

1. Wash and cut fruits into bite-sized pieces.
2. Slide the fruit pieces onto the skewers to create colorful fruit kabobs.

## 2. Ants on a Log:

Ingredients:

- Celery sticks
- Peanut butter or cream cheese
- Raisins

Steps:

1. Spread peanut butter or cream cheese inside celery sticks.
2. Place raisins on top, like "ants" marching on a log.

## 3. Mini Pizzas:

Ingredients:

- English muffins or small tortillas
- Pizza sauce
- Cheese (shredded)

- Toppings (e.g., sliced veggies, pepperoni)

Steps:

1. Spread pizza sauce on muffins or tortillas.
2. Add cheese and toppings.
3. Ask a grown-up to help bake them until the cheese melts.

## 4. Yogurt Parfait:

Ingredients:

- Yogurt (vanilla or fruit-flavored)
- Granola
- Fresh berries

Steps:

1. In a cup or bowl, layer yogurt, granola, and berries.
2. Repeat the layers to create a tasty parfait.

## 5. Apple Sandwiches:

Ingredients:

- Apple slices
- Peanut butter
- Raisins or chocolate chips

Steps:

1. Spread peanut butter on one apple slice.
2. Place another slice on top, making a "sandwich."
3. Press raisins or chocolate chips into the peanut butter.

## 6. Veggie Sticks with Dip:

Ingredients:

- Carrot sticks, cucumber slices, and bell pepper strips
- Hummus or ranch dip

Steps:

1. Wash and cut veggies into sticks or slices.
2. Dip them into hummus or ranch for a crunchy treat.

## 7. No-Bake Energy Bites:

Ingredients:

- Oats
- Peanut butter
- Honey
- Chocolate chips

Steps:

1. Mix oats, peanut butter, honey, and chocolate chips in a bowl.
2. Form small balls and refrigerate until firm.

## Remember:

- Always wash hands before cooking.
- If using the oven or stove, have a grown-up help with the hot stuff.

These snacks are not only delicious but also allow little chefs to get creative in the kitchen. Plus, they provide an opportunity to learn about different ingredients and kitchen skills in a fun and interactive way!

**What are 10 yummy parfaits you can make?**

## 1. Classic Berry Parfait:

- **Ingredients:** Greek yogurt, granola, fresh strawberries, and blueberries.
- **Steps:** Layer Greek yogurt, granola, and berries in a cup or bowl.

## 2. Chocolate Banana Crunch Parfait:

- **Ingredients:** Chocolate yogurt, banana slices, and chocolate granola.

- **Steps:** Alternate layers of chocolate yogurt, banana slices, and chocolate granola.

## 3. Tropical Paradise Parfait:

- **Ingredients:** Vanilla yogurt, diced pineapple, shredded coconut, and mango chunks.
- **Steps:** Layer vanilla yogurt, pineapple, coconut, and mango for a taste of the tropics.

## 4. Peanut Butter Banana Bliss Parfait:

- **Ingredients:** Peanut butter yogurt, banana slices, and crushed graham crackers.
- **Steps:** Create layers with peanut butter yogurt, banana slices, and a sprinkle of crushed graham crackers.

## 5. Strawberry Shortcake Parfait:

- **Ingredients:** Vanilla pudding, sliced strawberries, and shortbread cookie crumbles.
- **Steps:** Layer vanilla pudding, strawberries, and shortbread crumbles for a delightful treat.

## 6. Mango Raspberry Delight Parfait:

- **Ingredients:** Mango yogurt, fresh raspberries, and almond slices.

- **Steps:** Alternate layers of mango yogurt, raspberries, and almond slices.

## 7. Caramel Apple Pie Parfait:

- **Ingredients:** Caramel yogurt, diced apples, and cinnamon granola.
- **Steps:** Layer caramel yogurt, diced apples, and sprinkle with cinnamon granola.

## 8. Cookies and Cream Dream Parfait:

- **Ingredients:** Cookies and cream-flavored yogurt, crushed chocolate cookies, and whipped cream.
- **Steps:** Create layers with cookies and cream yogurt, crushed cookies, and a dollop of whipped cream.

## 9. Cherry Almond Cheesecake Parfait:

- **Ingredients:** Vanilla cheesecake pudding, cherry pie filling, and chopped almonds.
- **Steps:** Layer vanilla cheesecake pudding, cherry pie filling, and sprinkle with chopped almonds.

## 10. Rainbow Fruit Fiesta Parfait:

- **Ingredients:** Layers of various colored fruits like kiwi, pineapple, blueberries, and raspberries.

- **Steps:** Create a colorful parfait by layering different fruits for a fruity fiesta!

## Remember:

- Let little chefs have fun with the layers and combinations.
- Adjust ingredient quantities based on personal preferences.
- Use clear cups or glasses for a visually appealing presentation.

These simplified parfait ideas provide a tasty and visually appealing way for little chefs to explore different flavors and textures. Let creativity shine, and enjoy the delicious results!

## How do you make peanut butter and banana rolls?

Making peanut butter and banana rolls is a simple and tasty treat that little chefs can enjoy. Here's a simplified recipe for you:

## Peanut Butter and Banana Rolls:

**Ingredients:**

- 1 banana
- 2 tablespoons peanut butter
- 1 whole wheat tortilla

**Steps:**

1. **Prepare the Ingredients:**
   - Peel the banana.
   - Lay out a whole wheat tortilla on a clean surface.
2. **Spread Peanut Butter:**
   - Using a butter knife or spoon, spread a layer of peanut butter evenly over the entire surface of the tortilla.
3. **Place Banana on Tortilla:**
   - Place the peeled banana horizontally near one edge of the tortilla.
4. **Roll it Up:**
   - Carefully roll the tortilla around the banana, creating a snug roll. The peanut butter helps seal the edges.
5. **Slice into Rolls:**
   - Using a kid-friendly knife (under adult supervision), slice the rolled tortilla into bite-sized pieces, creating peanut butter and banana rolls.
6. **Serve and Enjoy:**
   - Arrange the rolls on a plate and enjoy your delicious peanut butter and banana treat!

# Variations:

- **Add a Drizzle:** Drizzle honey or a sprinkle of cinnamon on the banana before rolling for extra flavor.
- **Nutty Crunch:** Sprinkle crushed nuts (like almonds or walnuts) on the peanut butter before adding the banana.
- **Choco-Banana Rolls:** For a sweet twist, add a few chocolate chips before rolling.

## Tips for Little Chefs:

- Always wash your hands before preparing food.
- If using a knife, make sure it's kid-friendly and use it under adult supervision.
- Get creative with toppings and flavors!

This simple recipe not only introduces little chefs to basic kitchen skills but also provides a tasty and nutritious snack option. Enjoy your peanut butter and banana rolls!

**What are foodborne illnesses?**

Foodborne illnesses, simply put, are sicknesses caused by eating food contaminated with harmful germs or substances. These illnesses can make people feel unwell and can sometimes be serious. Here's a simplified explanation:

## What Are Foodborne Illnesses?

1. **Germ Invasion:**
   - Imagine tiny germs (like bacteria, viruses, or parasites) as sneaky invaders.
2. **Contaminated Food:**
   - Sometimes, these germs get into the food we eat, often because of poor hygiene during cooking or handling.
3. **Sickness Time:**
   - When we eat the contaminated food, these germs start causing trouble in our bodies.
4. **Common Symptoms:**
   - Feeling sick, stomachache, vomiting, diarrhea — these are common signs that our bodies are fighting off these unwelcome invaders.
5. **Types of Germs:**
   - Germs can be different types, like the ones that love to party in raw meat, unclean water, or uncooked eggs.

## Why It's Important to Avoid Foodborne Illnesses:

1. **Stay Healthy:**

- Nobody likes feeling sick! Avoiding foodborne illnesses helps us stay healthy and full of energy.

2. **Clean Hands, Safe Food:**
   - Washing hands, cooking food thoroughly, and keeping kitchen tools clean are like shields against these germs.

3. **Food Adventure Safety:**
   - Exploring new foods is fun! Knowing how to handle and cook them keeps our food adventures safe.

## Tips to Prevent Foodborne Illnesses:

1. **Wash Hands:**
   - Always wash hands before cooking or eating.

2. **Cook Thoroughly:**
   - Cook meat, poultry, and eggs thoroughly to kill germs.

3. **Separate Raw and Cooked:**
   - Keep raw meat separate from other foods to prevent cross-contamination.

4. **Clean Surfaces:**
   - Clean and sanitize kitchen surfaces and utensils regularly.

5. **Chill and Refrigerate:**
   - Refrigerate perishable foods promptly to slow down the growth of germs.

6. **Avoid Raw Eggs:**
    - Skip tasting raw cookie dough or licking the cake batter bowl if it has raw eggs.

# Conclusion:

Understanding foodborne illnesses is like having a superhero shield against invisible villains. By following simple kitchen rules and practicing good hygiene, little chefs can make sure their food adventures are not only delicious but also safe and healthy!

**What does cross-contamination mean?**

Cross-contamination is like when different foods accidentally share their germs, creating a sneaky way for those germs to spread. Let's simplify it:

# Cross-Contamination Explained:

1. **Germ Adventure:**
    - Imagine little germs on raw foods, like chicken or veggies. They're on an adventure!
2. **Meeting Point:**
    - If these germs from one food meet another food, it's like a secret meeting point for them.

3. **Spreading Sneakiness:**
   - Now, the germs can sneak onto the other food, making it a bit risky to eat without cooking.
4. **Example:**
   - If you cut raw chicken on a chopping board and then use the same board for veggies without cleaning it, the chicken germs can visit the veggies.

## Why It Matters:

1. **Safety First:**
   - Cross-contamination can spread harmful germs, making people sick if they eat the contaminated food.
2. **Cooking Can Save the Day:**
   - Cooking food thoroughly kills these germs, but we want to keep our kitchen clean to make cooking safe.

## How to Avoid Cross-Contamination:

1. **Separate Spaces:**
   - Use different cutting boards and utensils for raw meat and fresh produce.
2. **Handwashing Magic:**

- Wash hands after handling raw meat or eggs, so germs don't hitch a ride elsewhere.

3. **Clean and Wipe:**
   - Regularly clean surfaces, cutting boards, and utensils, especially if they touched raw stuff.
4. **Store Smart:**
   - Keep raw meat away from ready-to-eat foods in the fridge.
5. **Be Cautious with Towels:**
   - Avoid using the same towel for wiping hands and cleaning surfaces.

## In Short:

- Cross-contamination is like a game of tag for germs. To keep everyone safe and healthy, we play by the rules: separate, clean, and cook!

Understanding and avoiding cross-contamination is a key part of being a kitchen superhero, ensuring that our meals are not only tasty but also safe to eat.

**Here are some simple crockpot (slow cooker) recipes that little chefs can prepare with the help of grown-ups. Each recipe is simplified for easy understanding:**

# 1. Chicken and Veggie Stew:

- **Ingredients:**
    - Chicken pieces
    - Carrots, potatoes, and peas
    - Chicken broth
- **Steps:**
    1. Place chicken and veggies in the crockpot.
    2. Pour chicken broth over them.
    3. Cook on low for 6 hours.

# 2. Spaghetti Bolognese:

- **Ingredients:**
    - Ground beef
    - Spaghetti sauce
    - Diced tomatoes
    - Spaghetti noodles
- **Steps:**
    1. Brown beef in a pan.
    2. Transfer beef, sauce, and tomatoes to the crockpot.
    3. Cook on low for 4-6 hours.

# 3. Mac 'n' Cheese Delight:

- **Ingredients:**
    - Elbow macaroni
    - Cheddar cheese

    - Milk
- **Steps:**
    1. Mix macaroni, cheese, and milk in the crockpot.
    2. Cook on low for 2 hours.

# 4. Veggie Chili:

- **Ingredients:**
    - Kidney beans, black beans, corn
    - Diced tomatoes
    - Chili powder
- **Steps:**
    1. Combine all ingredients in the crockpot.
    2. Cook on low for 4-6 hours.

# 5. Teriyaki Chicken Bowl:

- **Ingredients:**
    - Chicken breasts
    - Teriyaki sauce
    - Broccoli florets
- **Steps:**
    1. Place chicken and broccoli in the crockpot.
    2. Pour teriyaki sauce over them.
    3. Cook on low for 4 hours.

# 6. Sloppy Joes:

- **Ingredients:**
  - Ground beef
  - Tomato sauce
  - Brown sugar
- **Steps:**
  1. Brown beef in a pan.
  2. Transfer beef, sauce, and sugar to the crockpot.
  3. Cook on low for 3-4 hours.

## 7. Sweet and Tangy Meatballs:

- **Ingredients:**
  - Frozen meatballs
  - Grape jelly
  - Barbecue sauce
- **Steps:**
  1. Mix meatballs, jelly, and sauce in the crockpot.
  2. Cook on low for 2-3 hours.

## 8. Vegetarian Lentil Soup:

- **Ingredients:**
  - Lentils, carrots, celery
  - Vegetable broth
- **Steps:**
  1. Combine ingredients in the crockpot.
  2. Cook on low for 6-8 hours.

## 9. Potato Broccoli Casserole:

- **Ingredients:**
    - Potatoes, broccoli
    - Cheddar cheese
    - Cream of mushroom soup
- **Steps:**
    1. Layer potatoes, broccoli, and cheese in the crockpot.
    2. Pour soup over the layers.
    3. Cook on low for 4-6 hours.

## 10. Rice Pudding Surprise:

- **Ingredients:**
    - White rice
    - Milk, sugar, cinnamon
- **Steps:**
    1. Mix rice, milk, sugar, and cinnamon in the crockpot.
    2. Cook on low for 2-3 hours.

## Tips for Little Chefs:

- Always have a grown-up help with hot and sharp things.
- Follow the steps and have fun experimenting with flavors!

These simplified crockpot recipes offer a variety of flavors and ingredients, making cooking an exciting and tasty adventure for little chefs!

## 11. Chicken and Rice Casserole:

- **Ingredients:**
    - Chicken thighs
    - White rice
    - Mixed vegetables (frozen)
    - Chicken broth
- **Steps:**
    1. Place chicken, rice, and veggies in the crockpot.
    2. Pour chicken broth over them.
    3. Cook on low for 4-6 hours.

## 12. Pulled Pork Sandwiches:

- **Ingredients:**
    - Pork shoulder
    - Barbecue sauce
    - Hamburger buns
- **Steps:**
    1. Place pork in the crockpot.
    2. Pour barbecue sauce over it.
    3. Cook on low for 8 hours.
    4. Shred pork and serve on buns.

## 13. Creamy Tomato Soup:

- **Ingredients:**
    - Canned tomatoes
    - Chicken broth
    - Cream
- **Steps:**
    1. Combine tomatoes and broth in the crockpot.
    2. Cook on low for 4 hours.
    3. Stir in cream before serving.

## 14. Beef and Vegetable Stew:

- **Ingredients:**
    - Stew beef
    - Potatoes, carrots, onions
    - Beef broth
- **Steps:**
    1. Place beef and veggies in the crockpot.
    2. Pour beef broth over them.
    3. Cook on low for 6-8 hours.

## 15. Cheesy Chicken and Broccoli:

- **Ingredients:**
    - Chicken breasts
    - Broccoli florets
    - Cheddar cheese

- **Steps:**
    1. Layer chicken and broccoli in the crockpot.
    2. Sprinkle cheese on top.
    3. Cook on low for 4 hours.

## 16. Lemon Garlic Chicken:

- **Ingredients:**
    - Chicken thighs
    - Garlic, lemon juice
    - Chicken broth
- **Steps:**
    1. Place chicken in the crockpot.
    2. Mix garlic, lemon juice, and broth; pour over the chicken.
    3. Cook on low for 5 hours.

## 17. Turkey and Vegetable Chili:

- **Ingredients:**
    - Ground turkey
    - Kidney beans, corn
    - Chili seasoning
- **Steps:**
    1. Brown turkey in a pan.
    2. Transfer turkey, beans, corn, and seasoning to the crockpot.
    3. Cook on low for 4-6 hours.

## 18. Sausage and Pepper Pasta:

- **Ingredients:**
    - Italian sausage
    - Bell peppers, onion
    - Marinara sauce
- **Steps:**
    1. Brown sausage in a pan.
    2. Transfer sausage, peppers, onion, and sauce to the crockpot.
    3. Cook on low for 4 hours.
    4. Serve over cooked pasta.

## 19. Teriyaki Beef Stir-Fry:

- **Ingredients:**
    - Beef strips
    - Broccoli, bell peppers
    - Teriyaki sauce
- **Steps:**
    1. Place beef and veggies in the crockpot.
    2. Pour teriyaki sauce over them.
    3. Cook on low for 4 hours.
    4. Serve over rice.

## 20. Chocolate Fondue:

- **Ingredients:**
    - Chocolate chips

- • Heavy cream
- • Dipping items (fruit, marshmallows)
- **Steps:**
  1. Mix chocolate chips and cream in the crockpot.
  2. Cook on low for 1-2 hours, stirring occasionally.
  3. Dip and enjoy!

# 21. Vegetarian Lentil Sloppy Joes:

- **Ingredients:**
  - • Lentils, rinsed
  - • Tomato sauce
  - • Bell peppers, diced
  - • Whole wheat buns
- **Steps:**
  1. Combine lentils, tomato sauce, and bell peppers in the crockpot.
  2. Cook on low for 6 hours.
  3. Serve on whole wheat buns.

# 22. Creamy Chicken and Rice Soup:

- **Ingredients:**
  - • Chicken broth
  - • Chicken breasts, diced

- Carrots, celery, rice
    - Cream of chicken soup
- **Steps:**
    1. Mix all ingredients in the crockpot.
    2. Cook on low for 6 hours.

# 23. BBQ Chicken Tacos:

- **Ingredients:**
    - Chicken thighs
    - BBQ sauce
    - Tortillas
    - Shredded lettuce, cheese (for toppings)
- **Steps:**
    1. Place chicken in the crockpot.
    2. Pour BBQ sauce over it.
    3. Cook on low for 4 hours.
    4. Shred chicken and serve in tortillas with toppings.

# 24. Honey Garlic Meatballs:

- **Ingredients:**
    - Frozen meatballs
    - Honey, soy sauce
    - Garlic, minced
- **Steps:**
    1. Mix honey, soy sauce, and garlic in the crockpot.

2. Add frozen meatballs.
3. Cook on low for 2-3 hours.

## 25. Buffalo Chicken Dip:

- **Ingredients:**
    - Cooked chicken, shredded
    - Cream cheese
    - Buffalo sauce
    - Shredded cheddar cheese
- **Steps:**
    1. Combine chicken, cream cheese, and buffalo sauce in the crockpot.
    2. Cook on low for 1-2 hours.
    3. Sprinkle cheddar cheese on top before serving.

## 26. Vegetarian Quinoa Chili:

- **Ingredients:**
    - Quinoa, rinsed
    - Black beans, corn, diced tomatoes
    - Chili seasoning
- **Steps:**
    1. Mix all ingredients in the crockpot.
    2. Cook on low for 4-6 hours.

## 27. Cheesy Broccoli and Rice Casserole:

- **Ingredients:**

- Broccoli florets
      - White rice
      - Cheddar cheese
      - Cream of mushroom soup
  - **Steps:**
    1. Layer broccoli, rice, and cheese in the crockpot.
    2. Pour soup over the layers.
    3. Cook on low for 3-4 hours.

## 28. Pasta with Marinara Sauce:

  - **Ingredients:**
      - Pasta sauce
      - Pasta of choice
      - Ground beef (optional)
  - **Steps:**
    1. If using beef, brown it in a pan.
    2. Transfer sauce, pasta, and beef (if using) to the crockpot.
    3. Cook on low for 2-3 hours.

## 29. Turkey and Sweet Potato Chili:

  - **Ingredients:**
      - Ground turkey
      - Sweet potatoes, diced
      - Black beans, diced tomatoes
      - Chili seasoning

- **Steps:**
    1. Brown turkey in a pan.
    2. Transfer turkey, sweet potatoes, beans, tomatoes, and seasoning to the crockpot.
    3. Cook on low for 4-6 hours.

# 30. Cranberry Orange Chicken:

- **Ingredients:**
    - Chicken breasts
    - Cranberry sauce
    - Orange juice
- **Steps:**
    1. Place chicken in the crockpot.
    2. Mix cranberry sauce and orange juice; pour over chicken.
    3. Cook on low for 4-5 hours.

# 31. Teriyaki Meatball Bowls:

- **Ingredients:**
    - Frozen meatballs
    - Teriyaki sauce
    - Cooked rice
    - Steamed broccoli
- **Steps:**
    1. Place frozen meatballs in the crockpot.
    2. Pour teriyaki sauce over them.
    3. Cook on low for 2-3 hours.

4. Serve over cooked rice with steamed broccoli.

## 32. Apple Cinnamon Oatmeal:

- **Ingredients:**
    - Rolled oats
    - Apples, diced
    - Cinnamon
    - Milk
- **Steps:**
    1. Combine oats, apples, cinnamon, and milk in the crockpot.
    2. Cook on low for 2-3 hours.
    3. Stir before serving.

## 33. Lemon Herb Chicken Drumsticks:

- **Ingredients:**
    - Chicken drumsticks
    - Lemon juice
    - Garlic powder, dried herbs
- **Steps:**
    1. Place chicken drumsticks in the crockpot.
    2. Mix lemon juice and herbs; pour over the chicken.
    3. Cook on low for 4-5 hours.

## 34. Broccoli Cheese Soup:

- **Ingredients:**
  - Broccoli florets
  - Cheddar cheese
  - Chicken broth
  - Cream of broccoli soup
- **Steps:**
  1. Combine broccoli, cheese, broth, and soup in the crockpot.
  2. Cook on low for 4 hours.

## 35. Hawaiian Pulled Pork Tacos:

- **Ingredients:**
  - Pork shoulder
  - Pineapple chunks
  - Barbecue sauce
  - Tortillas
- **Steps:**
  1. Place pork in the crockpot.
  2. Add pineapple chunks and barbecue sauce.
  3. Cook on low for 8 hours.
  4. Shred pork and serve in tortillas.

## 36. Creamy Tomato Basil Soup:

- **Ingredients:**
  - Canned tomatoes
  - Chicken broth
  - Fresh basil

- Heavy cream
- **Steps:**
    1. Combine tomatoes, broth, and basil in the crockpot.
    2. Cook on low for 4-6 hours.
    3. Stir in heavy cream before serving.

# 37. Pineapple Chicken Skewers:

- **Ingredients:**
    - Chicken breast chunks
    - Pineapple chunks
    - Soy sauce, honey
- **Steps:**
    1. Thread chicken and pineapple onto skewers.
    2. Mix soy sauce and honey; pour over skewers in the crockpot.
    3. Cook on low for 3-4 hours.

# 38. Butternut Squash Soup:

- **Ingredients:**
    - Butternut squash, peeled and diced
    - Onion, diced
    - Vegetable broth
    - Coconut milk
- **Steps:**

1. Combine squash, onion, broth, and coconut milk in the crockpot.
2. Cook on low for 6 hours.
3. Blend until smooth before serving.

## 39. Chickpea Curry:

- **Ingredients:**
    - Canned chickpeas
    - Curry powder, cumin
    - Coconut milk
- **Steps:**
    1. Mix chickpeas, curry powder, cumin, and coconut milk in the crockpot.
    2. Cook on low for 4-6 hours.
    3. Serve over rice.

## 40. Tomato Basil Chicken Pasta:

- **Ingredients:**
    - Chicken breasts
    - Tomato sauce
    - Fresh basil
    - Cooked pasta
- **Steps:**
    1. Place chicken in the crockpot.
    2. Pour tomato sauce over it.
    3. Cook on low for 4-5 hours.
    4. Shred chicken and serve over cooked pasta.

# Tips for Little Chefs:

- Ask for help with handling hot items.
- Experiment with adding your favorite ingredients.
- Enjoy the process and share your delicious creations!

These crockpot recipes offer a mix of flavors and ingredients, providing little chefs with a variety of options to explore in the kitchen. Happy cooking!

**How do you boil pasta? How do you know when its cooked? What does al dente mean?**

Boiling pasta is a simple process, and testing it for doneness is key to achieving the desired texture, especially "al dente." Let's break it down in a simplified way:

## Boiling Pasta:

1. **Boil Water:**
   - Fill a pot with water. Use about 4-6 quarts of water for every pound of pasta.
2. **Add Salt (Optional):**
   - Add a pinch of salt to the boiling water. This adds flavor to the pasta.

3. **Add Pasta:**
   - Gently add the pasta to the boiling water. Stir immediately to prevent sticking.
4. **Stir Occasionally:**
   - Stir the pasta occasionally while it cooks to ensure even cooking and prevent clumping.
5. **Check Cooking Time:**
   - Follow the package instructions for cooking time. It usually ranges from 8 to 12 minutes.
6. **Taste Test:**
   - About 1-2 minutes before the suggested cooking time is up, start tasting a piece of pasta to check for doneness.

## Testing Pasta Doneness (Al Dente):

- **Look for Firmness:**
  - Al dente means "to the tooth" in Italian. It refers to pasta that is cooked but still has a bit of firmness when bitten.
- **Take a Bite:**
  - Bite into a small piece of pasta. It should be tender but have a slight resistance when you bite it.
- **No Raw Flour Taste:**
  - There should be no raw flour taste, but the center of the pasta should not be completely soft.

- **Check Color:**
    - The pasta should have a consistent color throughout. If it's still white in the center, it needs more time.

## How to Drain:

1. **Use a Strainer:**
    - Once the pasta is al dente, turn off the heat and carefully pour the pasta into a colander or strainer in the sink.
2. **Save Some Pasta Water:**
    - Before draining, reserve a cup of the pasta cooking water. It can be used to adjust the consistency of your sauce later.
3. **Rinse (Optional):**
    - Some people prefer to rinse the pasta under cold water to stop the cooking process and cool it down quickly, especially for cold salads. However, for hot dishes, this step is often skipped.

## Tips for Little Chefs:

- Always have a grown-up help with handling hot water and using the stove.
- Experiment with different pasta shapes and types.
- Enjoy the pasta with your favorite sauce or toppings!

By testing for al dente, you'll ensure that your pasta has a delightful texture, neither too soft nor too firm, making it perfect for various dishes.

**How do you cook spaghetti and meatballs using frozen meatballs?**

Cooking spaghetti and meatballs using frozen meatballs is a convenient and quick way to prepare a delicious meal. Here's a simplified guide for little chefs:

## Ingredients:

- Frozen meatballs
- Spaghetti noodles
- Tomato sauce (store-bought or homemade)
- Grated Parmesan cheese (optional)

## Instructions:

1. **Boil Water for Pasta:**
   - Ask a grown-up to help you bring a large pot of water to a boil. Add a pinch of salt if you like.
2. **Add Spaghetti:**
   - Gently place the spaghetti noodles into the boiling water. Cook according to the

package instructions (usually around 8-10 minutes).

3. **Heat Tomato Sauce:**
   - While the pasta is cooking, pour the tomato sauce into a separate saucepan. Heat it on the stove over medium heat.

4. **Add Frozen Meatballs:**
   - Drop the frozen meatballs into the simmering tomato sauce. Stir occasionally to coat them in the sauce.

5. **Cook Meatballs:**
   - Let the meatballs cook in the sauce for about 10-15 minutes, or according to the package instructions. They will heat through and absorb the delicious flavors of the sauce.

6. **Check Pasta Doneness:**
   - Taste a small piece of spaghetti to check if it's cooked to your liking. It should be al dente—cooked but still slightly firm when bitten.

7. **Drain Pasta:**
   - Once the pasta is done, carefully ask for help to drain it using a colander in the sink.

8. **Serve:**
   - Place a portion of spaghetti on each plate, and ladle the tomato sauce and meatballs over the top. If you like, sprinkle some grated Parmesan cheese on top.

9. **Enjoy:**
    - Now, it's time to enjoy your spaghetti and meatballs! Don't forget to slurp the noodles and savor the tasty meatballs.

## Tips for Little Chefs:

- Always have a grown-up help with boiling water and using the stove.
- Feel free to customize your meal with extra toppings like more cheese, herbs, or a sprinkle of black pepper.
- Ask for help if you need to cut or handle anything hot.

This simplified recipe allows little chefs to enjoy a classic and hearty meal with the convenience of frozen meatballs. Enjoy your delicious spaghetti and meatballs!

**How do you make meatball subs using frozen meatballs?**

Making meatball subs using frozen meatballs is a simple and delicious process. Here's a simplified guide for little chefs:

# Ingredients:

- Frozen meatballs
- Submarine rolls or baguette
- Tomato sauce (store-bought or homemade)
- Mozzarella cheese, shredded
- Grated Parmesan cheese (optional)
- Dried oregano or Italian seasoning (optional)

## Instructions:

1. **Preheat the Oven:**
   - Ask a grown-up to preheat the oven according to the package instructions for the frozen meatballs (usually around 350°F or 180°C).
2. **Bake the Meatballs:**
   - Place the frozen meatballs on a baking sheet. Follow the package instructions for baking time. Usually, it takes around 15-20 minutes.
3. **Warm Tomato Sauce:**
   - While the meatballs are baking, heat the tomato sauce in a saucepan on the stove. Simmer it over low heat.
4. **Slice the Rolls:**
   - Ask for help to slice the submarine rolls or baguette in half, creating a pocket for the meatballs.
5. **Assemble the Subs:**

- Once the meatballs are fully cooked, place them in the sliced rolls.

6. **Add Tomato Sauce:**
   - Spoon warm tomato sauce over the meatballs, ensuring they are generously coated.

7. **Sprinkle with Cheese:**
   - Sprinkle shredded mozzarella cheese over the meatballs and tomato sauce. If you like, add a bit of grated Parmesan cheese on top.

8. **Bake in the Oven:**
   - Place the assembled meatball subs back in the oven for a few minutes, just until the cheese melts and becomes gooey.

9. **Optional: Add Seasonings:**
   - If you have dried oregano or Italian seasoning, sprinkle a bit over the top for extra flavor.

10. **Serve:**
    - Carefully take the meatball subs out of the oven, and let them cool for a moment. Then, serve them on plates.

11. **Enjoy:**
    - Dive into your delicious meatball subs! The warm, cheesy, saucy goodness is ready to be enjoyed.

# Tips for Little Chefs:

- Always have a grown-up help with using the oven and handling hot items.
- Feel free to add more toppings like sliced olives, green peppers, or your favorite sauces.
- Share the meal with friends or family for a fun and tasty gathering.

This simplified recipe lets little chefs create a classic and satisfying meal with the convenience of frozen meatballs. Enjoy your meatball subs!

## How do I make barbeque little smokies or meatballs?

Making BBQ little smokies or meatballs is a simple and tasty process. Here's a simplified guide for little chefs:

## BBQ Little Smokies:

Ingredients:

- Little smokies (mini sausages)
- BBQ sauce
- Toothpicks (optional)

Instructions:

1. **Prepare Little Smokies:**

- If the little smokies are frozen, heat them according to the package instructions. If they're already cooked, you can proceed to the next step.

2. **Add BBQ Sauce:**
    - Place the little smokies in a bowl, and pour your favorite BBQ sauce over them. Use enough sauce to coat each little smokie.

3. **Mix and Coat:**
    - Gently toss the little smokies in the BBQ sauce until they are well coated.

4. **Heat on the Stove or Slow Cooker:**
    - Warm the BBQ-coated little smokies on the stove over low heat or in a slow cooker for about 1-2 hours. This allows the flavors to meld together.

5. **Serve:**
    - Skewer the little smokies with toothpicks for easy serving, or simply place them in a bowl. Enjoy your BBQ little smokies!

## BBQ Meatballs:

Ingredients:

- Frozen meatballs (homemade or store-bought)
- BBQ sauce
- Toothpicks (optional)

Instructions:

1. **Bake Meatballs:**
   - If the meatballs are frozen, bake them according to the package instructions until fully cooked.
2. **Coat with BBQ Sauce:**
   - In a bowl, toss the cooked meatballs with your favorite BBQ sauce until they are evenly coated.
3. **Simmer in BBQ Sauce:**
   - Place the BBQ-coated meatballs in a saucepan on the stove over low heat. Let them simmer in the BBQ sauce for about 15-20 minutes to absorb the flavor.
4. **Serve:**
   - Skewer the BBQ meatballs with toothpicks for easy serving, or serve them in a bowl. Your BBQ meatballs are ready to be enjoyed!

## Tips for Little Chefs:

- Always have a grown-up help with using the stove or oven and handling hot items.
- Feel free to customize the level of BBQ sauce according to your taste preferences.
- Enjoy your BBQ little smokies or meatballs as a snack or part of a meal.

This simplified recipe lets little chefs create a flavorful and fun BBQ dish. Enjoy your delicious BBQ little smokies or meatballs!

## What are pigs in a blanket and how do you make them?

"Pigs in a blanket" is a fun and popular snack where small sausages or hot dogs are wrapped in a layer of dough and baked until golden brown. Here's a simplified guide for little chefs:

## Ingredients:

- Cocktail sausages or hot dogs
- Crescent roll dough (store-bought)
- Optional: Cheese slices (for extra flavor)

## Instructions:

1. **Preheat the Oven:**
   - Ask a grown-up to help preheat the oven according to the crescent roll dough package instructions (usually around 375°F or 190°C).
2. **Prepare Sausages or Hot Dogs:**

- If using hot dogs, you can slice them into smaller pieces. If using cocktail sausages, they are usually ready to go.

3. **Unroll Crescent Roll Dough:**
   - Open the package of crescent roll dough and carefully unroll it on a clean surface.

4. **Separate Dough Triangles:**
   - Crescent roll dough usually comes in perforated triangles. Gently separate these triangles.

5. **Wrap Sausages:**
   - Take each sausage or hot dog piece and place it at the wide end of a dough triangle. Roll it up towards the point, completely covering the sausage.

6. **Place on Baking Sheet:**
   - Arrange the wrapped sausages on a baking sheet, leaving a little space between each one.

7. **Optional: Add Cheese:**
   - If you like, you can add a small slice of cheese before wrapping the sausage in the dough for extra flavor.

8. **Bake in the Oven:**
   - Carefully place the baking sheet in the preheated oven and bake according to the crescent roll dough package instructions. Usually, it takes around 10-12 minutes or until the dough is golden brown.

9. **Cool and Serve:**
    - Once baked, let the pigs in a blanket cool for a few minutes. They can be enjoyed on their own or with your favorite dipping sauce.

## Tips for Little Chefs:

- Always have a grown-up help with using the oven and handling hot items.
- Experiment with different types of sausages or hot dogs for variety.
- Get creative with dipping sauces like ketchup, mustard, or a cheese dip.

Pigs in a blanket are a delightful and easy-to-make snack that's perfect for parties or as a tasty treat. Enjoy making and eating these bite-sized delights!

### How to properly fry a breaded porkchop?

Frying a breaded pork chop is a delicious and simple way to prepare this classic dish. Here's a simplified recipe for little chefs:

## Ingredients:

- Pork chops (bone-in or boneless)

- Bread crumbs (store-bought or homemade)
- All-purpose flour
- Eggs
- Salt and pepper
- Cooking oil (vegetable or canola oil)

## Instructions:

1. **Prepare the Breading Station:**
   - Set up a breading station with three shallow dishes. In one dish, put flour; in the second, beat the eggs; and in the third, place the bread crumbs. Season the flour and bread crumbs with a pinch of salt and pepper.
2. **Dredge the Pork Chops:**
   - Dip each pork chop into the flour, coating it on both sides. Shake off any excess flour. Then, dip it into the beaten eggs, ensuring it's well coated. Finally, press the pork chop into the bread crumbs, making sure it's evenly covered.
3. **Heat the Oil:**
   - Ask a grown-up to help you heat the cooking oil in a large skillet over medium-high heat. You want enough oil to cover the bottom of the pan.
4. **Fry the Pork Chops:**

- Once the oil is hot, carefully place the breaded pork chops in the skillet. Cook them for about 4-6 minutes per side, or until they are golden brown and the internal temperature reaches 145°F (63°C) for pork.

5. **Drain on Paper Towels:**
    - Use tongs to transfer the fried pork chops to a plate lined with paper towels. This helps absorb any excess oil.

6. **Check for Doneness:**
    - If you have a meat thermometer, you can check the internal temperature of the pork chops to ensure they are cooked through.

7. **Serve:**
    - Let the pork chops rest for a few minutes before serving. This helps the juices redistribute, keeping the meat moist. Serve with your favorite sides.

## Tips for Little Chefs:

- Always have a grown-up help with using the stove and handling hot oil.
- Be careful not to overcrowd the pan; fry a few pork chops at a time to maintain an even temperature.
- You can add your favorite herbs or spices to the flour or bread crumbs for extra flavor.

This simplified recipe allows little chefs to enjoy the crispy and flavorful goodness of breaded pork chops. Enjoy your delicious meal!

**What are 10 casseroles little chefs can bake?**

Here are 10 simplified casserole recipes that little chefs can bake with the help of grown-ups:

# 1. Cheesy Chicken and Broccoli Casserole:

- **Ingredients:**
    - Cooked chicken, diced
    - Broccoli florets
    - Cheddar cheese
    - Cream of chicken soup
- **Instructions:**
    1. Mix chicken, broccoli, and cheese in a bowl.
    2. Stir in cream of chicken soup.
    3. Transfer to a baking dish and bake at 350°F (180°C) for 25-30 minutes.

# 2. Taco Casserole:

- **Ingredients:**
    - Ground beef, cooked

- Taco seasoning
- Black beans, corn
- Shredded cheddar cheese

- **Instructions:**
  1. Mix beef, taco seasoning, beans, and corn.
  2. Layer in a baking dish and top with cheese.
  3. Bake at 375°F (190°C) for 20-25 minutes.

# 3. Vegetarian Quinoa Casserole:

- **Ingredients:**
  - Quinoa, cooked
  - Black beans, diced tomatoes
  - Corn, bell peppers
  - Shredded mozzarella
- **Instructions:**
  1. Mix quinoa, beans, tomatoes, corn, and peppers.
  2. Top with mozzarella and bake at 350°F (180°C) for 25 minutes.

# 4. Classic Tuna Noodle Casserole:

- **Ingredients:**
  - Egg noodles, cooked
  - Canned tuna
  - Frozen peas
  - Cream of mushroom soup
- **Instructions:**

1. Mix noodles, tuna, peas, and soup.
2. Bake at 375°F (190°C) for 20-25 minutes.

## 5. Breakfast Casserole:

- **Ingredients:**
    - Hash browns
    - Eggs, beaten
    - Sausage, cooked and crumbled
    - Shredded cheddar cheese
- **Instructions:**
    1. Layer hash browns, sausage, and cheese in a baking dish.
    2. Pour beaten eggs over the layers.
    3. Bake at 350°F (180°C) for 30-35 minutes.

## 6. Broccoli and Rice Casserole:

- **Ingredients:**
    - Cooked rice
    - Broccoli florets
    - Cheddar cheese
    - Cream of broccoli soup
- **Instructions:**
    1. Mix rice, broccoli, and cheese.
    2. Stir in cream of broccoli soup.
    3. Bake at 375°F (190°C) for 20-25 minutes.

## 7. Sloppy Joe Casserole:

- **Ingredients:**
    - Ground beef, cooked
    - Sloppy Joe sauce
    - Cornbread mix
    - Shredded cheddar cheese
- **Instructions:**
    1. Mix beef with Sloppy Joe sauce.
    2. Prepare cornbread mix and spread over the beef.
    3. Top with cheese and bake at 375°F (190°C) for 20-25 minutes.

# 8. Zucchini and Tomato Casserole:

- **Ingredients:**
    - Zucchini, sliced
    - Cherry tomatoes, halved
    - Parmesan cheese
    - Bread crumbs
- **Instructions:**
    1. Layer zucchini and tomatoes in a baking dish.
    2. Sprinkle with Parmesan and bread crumbs.
    3. Bake at 375°F (190°C) for 20 minutes.

# 9. Pizza Casserole:

- **Ingredients:**
    - Penne pasta, cooked

- Marinara sauce
- Pepperoni slices
- Mozzarella cheese
- **Instructions:**
  1. Mix pasta with marinara sauce and layer in a baking dish.
  2. Top with pepperoni and mozzarella.
  3. Bake at 375°F (190°C) for 20-25 minutes.

# 10. Chicken and Rice Casserole:

- **Ingredients:**
  - Cooked chicken, shredded
  - Cooked rice
  - Mixed vegetables (frozen)
  - Cream of chicken soup
- **Instructions:**
  1. Mix chicken, rice, and vegetables.
  2. Stir in cream of chicken soup.
  3. Bake at 350°F (180°C) for 25-30 minutes.

# 11. Baked Spaghetti Casserole:

- **Ingredients:**
  - Cooked spaghetti
  - Ground beef, cooked
  - Marinara sauce

- Ricotta cheese
- Shredded mozzarella
- **Instructions:**
  1. Mix spaghetti, beef, and marinara sauce.
  2. Layer in a baking dish with dollops of ricotta.
  3. Top with mozzarella and bake at 375°F (190°C) for 20-25 minutes.

## 12. Chili Mac and Cheese Casserole:

- **Ingredients:**
  - Cooked macaroni
  - Canned chili
  - Shredded cheddar cheese
  - Diced onions (optional)
- **Instructions:**
  1. Mix macaroni, chili, and onions.
  2. Layer in a baking dish and top with cheddar cheese.
  3. Bake at 375°F (190°C) for 20-25 minutes.

## 13. Spinach and Artichoke Chicken Casserole:

- **Ingredients:**
  - Cooked chicken, shredded
  - Frozen spinach, thawed and drained
  - Canned artichoke hearts, chopped

- Cream cheese
- **Instructions:**
    1. Mix chicken, spinach, artichokes, and cream cheese.
    2. Transfer to a baking dish and bake at 350°F (180°C) for 25-30 minutes.

# 14. Tater Tot Casserole:

- **Ingredients:**
    - Ground beef, cooked
    - Frozen tater tots
    - Cream of mushroom soup
    - Shredded cheddar cheese
- **Instructions:**
    1. Layer beef, tater tots, and soup in a baking dish.
    2. Top with cheddar cheese and bake at 375°F (190°C) for 25-30 minutes.

# 15. Egg and Sausage Breakfast Casserole:

- **Ingredients:**
    - Eggs, beaten
    - Breakfast sausage, cooked and crumbled
    - Bread cubes
    - Shredded cheddar cheese
- **Instructions:**
    1. Mix eggs, sausage, and bread cubes.

2.  Transfer to a baking dish and top with cheddar cheese.
3.  Bake at 350°F (180°C) for 30-35 minutes.

## 16. Sweet Potato and Black Bean Enchilada Casserole:

- **Ingredients:**
    - Sweet potatoes, diced and roasted
    - Black beans, drained and rinsed
    - Enchilada sauce
    - Shredded Monterey Jack cheese
- **Instructions:**
    1.  Layer sweet potatoes, black beans, and enchilada sauce in a baking dish.
    2.  Top with Monterey Jack cheese and bake at 375°F (190°C) for 20-25 minutes.

## 17. Buffalo Chicken Cauliflower Casserole:

- **Ingredients:**
    - Cooked chicken, shredded
    - Cauliflower florets, steamed
    - Buffalo sauce
    - Cream cheese
- **Instructions:**
    1.  Mix chicken, cauliflower, buffalo sauce, and cream cheese.

2. Transfer to a baking dish and bake at 350°F (180°C) for 25-30 minutes.

# 18. Ham and Cheese Hash Brown Casserole:

- **Ingredients:**
    - Frozen hash browns
    - Cooked ham, diced
    - Shredded cheddar cheese
    - Sour cream
- **Instructions:**
    1. Mix hash browns, ham, and sour cream.
    2. Layer in a baking dish and top with cheddar cheese.
    3. Bake at 375°F (190°C) for 30-35 minutes.

# 19. Mushroom and Swiss Chicken Casserole:

- **Ingredients:**
    - Cooked chicken, shredded
    - Mushrooms, sliced and sautéed
    - Swiss cheese, shredded
    - Cream of mushroom soup
- **Instructions:**
    1. Mix chicken, mushrooms, and soup.
    2. Transfer to a baking dish and top with Swiss cheese.

3. Bake at 350°F (180°C) for 25-30 minutes.

## 20. Cabbage Roll Casserole:

- **Ingredients:**
    - Ground beef, cooked
    - Cabbage, shredded
    - Rice, cooked
    - Tomato sauce
- **Instructions:**
    1. Mix beef, cabbage, rice, and half of the tomato sauce.
    2. Layer in a baking dish, pour remaining sauce on top.
    3. Bake at 375°F (190°C) for 30-35 minutes.

## Tips for Little Chefs:

- Always have a grown-up help with using the oven and handling hot dishes.
- Feel free to add your favorite ingredients or experiment with different flavors.
- Share these tasty casseroles with family and friends!

**How do you make a homemade pizza?**

Making homemade pizza can be a fun and tasty activity for little chefs! Here's a simplified recipe for making a basic homemade pizza:

## Ingredients:

Pizza Dough:

- 2 1/4 teaspoons (1 packet) active dry yeast
- 1 teaspoon sugar
- 1 cup warm water
- 2 1/2 to 3 cups all-purpose flour
- 1 tablespoon olive oil
- 1 teaspoon salt

Pizza Sauce:

- 1 can (14 ounces) crushed tomatoes
- 1 teaspoon dried oregano
- 1 teaspoon dried basil
- 1/2 teaspoon garlic powder
- Salt and pepper to taste

Toppings:

- Shredded mozzarella cheese
- Your favorite pizza toppings (e.g., pepperoni, sliced bell peppers, olives)

## Instructions:

1. **Prepare the Pizza Dough:**

   1. In a bowl, combine warm water, sugar, and yeast. Let it sit for about 5 minutes until it becomes frothy.
   2. Add olive oil and salt to the yeast mixture.
   3. Gradually add flour, stirring until a dough forms.
   4. Knead the dough on a floured surface for a few minutes until it becomes smooth.
   5. Place the dough in a lightly oiled bowl, cover with a cloth, and let it rise in a warm place for about 1 hour.

2. **Make the Pizza Sauce:**

   1. In a bowl, mix crushed tomatoes, oregano, basil, garlic powder, salt, and pepper.
   2. Taste and adjust the seasonings according to your preference.

3. **Preheat the Oven:**

   1. Ask a grown-up to help preheat the oven to 475°F (245°C). If you have a pizza stone, place it in the oven to heat.

4. **Roll Out the Dough:**

   1. On a floured surface, roll out the pizza dough to your desired thickness.

2. If you have a pizza peel, transfer the rolled-out dough onto it. Otherwise, use a baking sheet.

5. **Assemble the Pizza:**

   1. Spread a thin layer of pizza sauce over the dough, leaving a small border around the edges.
   2. Sprinkle shredded mozzarella cheese evenly over the sauce.
   3. Add your favorite toppings.

6. **Bake the Pizza:**

   1. If using a pizza stone, carefully transfer the pizza onto the hot stone in the oven. If using a baking sheet, place the sheet in the oven.
   2. Bake for 12-15 minutes or until the crust is golden and the cheese is melted and bubbly.

7. **Serve and Enjoy:**

   1. Carefully remove the pizza from the oven.
   2. Allow it to cool for a few minutes, then slice and enjoy your homemade pizza!

## Tips for Little Chefs:

- Always have a grown-up help with using the oven and handling hot items.
- Get creative with your toppings! Experiment with different cheeses, vegetables, and meats.

- Share the delicious pizza with your family and friends.

This simplified homemade pizza recipe allows little chefs to create their own personalized pizza with ease. Have fun and enjoy your tasty creation!

## How do I make chicken and dumplings?

Making chicken and dumplings is a comforting and delicious dish. Here's a simplified recipe for little chefs:

# Ingredients:

For the Chicken Stew:

- 2 cups cooked chicken, shredded (you can use rotisserie chicken)
- 4 cups chicken broth
- 2 carrots, peeled and sliced
- 2 celery stalks, sliced
- 1 onion, finely chopped
- 2 cloves garlic, minced
- 1 teaspoon dried thyme
- Salt and pepper to taste
- 2 tablespoons butter
- 2 tablespoons all-purpose flour
- 1/2 cup milk

For the Dumplings:

- 1 cup all-purpose flour
- 1 1/2 teaspoons baking powder
- 1/2 teaspoon salt
- 1/2 cup milk

## Instructions:

1. **Prepare the Chicken Stew:**

   1. In a large pot, melt butter over medium heat. Add chopped onions, garlic, carrots, and celery. Cook until the vegetables are slightly softened.
   2. Stir in the flour to create a roux. Cook for 1-2 minutes, stirring constantly.
   3. Gradually whisk in the chicken broth to avoid lumps. Bring it to a gentle boil.
   4. Add shredded chicken and dried thyme to the pot. Season with salt and pepper to taste.
   5. Reduce heat to simmer and let it cook for about 10-15 minutes, allowing the flavors to meld.
   6. Pour in the milk and stir. Allow the stew to simmer while you prepare the dumplings.

2. **Prepare the Dumplings:**

   1. In a mixing bowl, whisk together flour, baking powder, and salt.
   2. Gradually add milk to the dry ingredients, stirring until just combined. The dough will be thick and sticky.

3. **Add Dumplings to Stew:**

   1. Drop spoonfuls of dumpling dough onto the simmering chicken stew.
   2. Cover the pot with a lid and let the dumplings cook for 10-15 minutes, or until they are cooked through and fluffy. Resist the urge to lift the lid while the dumplings are cooking.

4. **Serve and Enjoy:**

   1. Once the dumplings are cooked, give the stew a gentle stir.
   2. Ladle the chicken and dumplings into bowls and enjoy your comforting homemade meal!

## Tips for Little Chefs:

- Always have a grown-up help with using the stove and handling hot items.
- Get creative by adding your favorite vegetables to the stew.
- You can also experiment with different herbs and seasonings to personalize the flavor.

This simplified chicken and dumplings recipe is perfect for little chefs to enjoy a warm and hearty dish. Dive into the deliciousness!

**What is a pizza burger and how do you make it?**

A pizza burger is a creative and delicious twist on the classic hamburger, combining the flavors of pizza with a juicy burger. Here's a simplified recipe for little chefs:

# Ingredients:

For the Burger Patties:

- 1 pound ground beef
- Salt and pepper to taste
- 1 teaspoon dried oregano
- 1 teaspoon garlic powder

For the Pizza Sauce:

- 1/2 cup tomato sauce
- 1 teaspoon dried oregano
- 1/2 teaspoon garlic powder
- Salt and pepper to taste

Other Ingredients:

- Burger buns
- Shredded mozzarella cheese
- Your favorite pizza toppings (e.g., pepperoni, sliced bell peppers, olives)

# Instructions:

1. **Prepare the Burger Patties:**

   1. In a bowl, mix ground beef with salt, pepper,
      dried oregano, and garlic powder.
   2. Divide the mixture into burger-sized patties.

2. **Cook the Burger Patties:**

   1. Ask a grown-up to help you cook the burger
      patties. You can grill them, cook them on a
      stovetop, or use a toaster oven.
   2. Cook the patties until they reach your desired
      level of doneness.

3. **Make the Pizza Sauce:**

   1. In a small bowl, mix tomato sauce with dried
      oregano, garlic powder, salt, and pepper.

4. **Assemble the Pizza Burgers:**

   1. Place the cooked burger patties on the bottom
      half of the burger buns.
   2. Spoon a dollop of pizza sauce over each patty.
   3. Sprinkle shredded mozzarella cheese on top of
      the sauce.
   4. Add your favorite pizza toppings to customize
      your pizza burger.

5. **Melt the Cheese:**

1. Place the assembled burger in a toaster oven or under a broiler for a few minutes, just until the cheese melts and becomes bubbly.

6. **Top and Serve:**

1. Place the top half of the burger bun on each pizza burger.
2. Serve your delicious pizza burgers hot and enjoy!

# Tips for Little Chefs:

- Always have a grown-up help with cooking and handling hot items.
- Get creative with your pizza toppings to make your pizza burger unique.
- Share your tasty creation with family and friends.

This simplified pizza burger recipe combines the best of both worlds – the savory goodness of a burger with the flavors of pizza. Have fun making and savoring your pizza burgers!

**How do you make yummy simple vegetables and what are the recipes? Why you need to eat more veggies?**

Eating more vegetables is essential for maintaining a healthy and balanced diet. Vegetables provide a wide range of vitamins, minerals, fiber, and antioxidants that contribute to overall well-being. Here are some simplified and yummy vegetable recipes along with the reasons why it's important to eat more veggies:

## Why Eat More Veggies:

1. **Nutrient Powerhouses:**
   - Vegetables are packed with essential vitamins and minerals, such as vitamin C, potassium, and folate, which play crucial roles in various bodily functions.
2. **Fiber Boost:**
   - Fiber in vegetables helps maintain a healthy digestive system, aids in weight management, and can contribute to lower cholesterol levels.
3. **Antioxidant Protection:**
   - Many vegetables are rich in antioxidants that help protect cells from damage, reduce inflammation, and support the immune system.
4. **Hydration and Satiety:**
   - Vegetables often have high water content, contributing to hydration. Additionally, the fiber in veggies can help you feel full, aiding in weight control.
5. **Disease Prevention:**
   - Regular consumption of vegetables has been linked to a lower risk of chronic

diseases such as heart disease, certain cancers, and type 2 diabetes.

# Simple and Yummy Vegetable Recipes:

1. **Roasted Vegetables:**

   - **Ingredients:**
     - Assorted vegetables (e.g., carrots, broccoli, bell peppers)
     - Olive oil
     - Salt and pepper
   - **Instructions:**
     1. Toss chopped vegetables with olive oil, salt, and pepper.
     2. Roast in the oven at 400°F (200°C) for 20-25 minutes or until tender.

2. **Stir-Fried Vegetables:**

   - **Ingredients:**
     - Mixed vegetables (e.g., broccoli, snow peas, carrots)
     - Soy sauce
     - Sesame oil
     - Garlic (minced)
   - **Instructions:**
     1. Stir-fry vegetables in a pan with garlic, soy sauce, and a touch of sesame oil until crisp-tender.

3. **Vegetable Skewers:**

- **Ingredients:**
    - Cherry tomatoes
    - Zucchini slices
    - Mushrooms
    - Bell pepper chunks
- **Instructions:**
    1. Thread vegetables onto skewers and grill or bake until lightly charred.

4. **Vegetable Omelets:**

- **Ingredients:**
    - Eggs
    - Spinach
    - Tomatoes
    - Onions
    - Bell peppers
- **Instructions:**
    1. Saute chopped vegetables, then pour beaten eggs over them to make a delicious omelet.

5. **Caprese Salad:**

- **Ingredients:**
    - Cherry tomatoes
    - Fresh mozzarella
    - Basil leaves

- Balsamic glaze
- **Instructions:**
  1. Arrange tomato and mozzarella slices with basil leaves. Drizzle with balsamic glaze.

6. **Vegetable Soup:**

- **Ingredients:**
  - Mixed vegetables (carrots, celery, potatoes)
  - Vegetable broth
  - Garlic and onion
  - Herbs (thyme, rosemary)
- **Instructions:**
  1. Saute garlic and onion, add chopped vegetables, herbs, and broth. Simmer until vegetables are tender.

# Tips for Little Chefs:

- Explore different colors and varieties of vegetables for a diverse range of nutrients.
- Involve kids in the preparation process to make eating veggies more enjoyable.
- Experiment with herbs and spices to add flavor without extra calories.

Remember, a variety of colorful vegetables on your plate is not only delicious but also a fantastic way to promote good health. Enjoy your veggie-filled meals!

## How do I make tasty green beans or cheesy broccoli?

 Here are simplified recipes for tasty green beans and cheesy broccoli:

## Tasty Green Beans:

Ingredients:

- Fresh green beans, washed and trimmed
- Olive oil
- Garlic powder
- Salt and pepper
- Lemon juice (optional)

Instructions:

1. **Blanch the Green Beans:**
   - Bring a pot of salted water to a boil. Add the green beans and cook for 2-3 minutes until they turn bright green. Quickly transfer them to a bowl of ice water to stop the cooking process.
2. **Sauté the Green Beans:**
   - Heat olive oil in a pan over medium heat. Add the blanched green beans and sauté for 2-3 minutes until they are tender-crisp.
3. **Season:**
   - Sprinkle garlic powder, salt, and pepper over the green beans. Toss to coat evenly.

4. **Finish with Lemon Juice (Optional):**
   - Squeeze fresh lemon juice over the green beans for a burst of freshness.
5. **Serve:**
   - Transfer the green beans to a serving dish. They are now ready to be enjoyed as a tasty and vibrant side dish.

# Cheesy Broccoli:

Ingredients:

- Broccoli florets
- Cheddar cheese, shredded
- Milk
- Butter
- All-purpose flour
- Salt and pepper

Instructions:

1. **Steam the Broccoli:**
   - Steam the broccoli until it's tender but still has a slight crunch. You can steam it on the stovetop or use a microwave-safe dish with a bit of water.
2. **Make the Cheese Sauce:**
   - In a saucepan, melt butter over medium heat. Stir in flour to create a roux.
3. **Add Milk:**

- Gradually whisk in milk, stirring constantly to avoid lumps. Continue cooking until the mixture thickens.

4. **Add Cheese:**
   - Reduce the heat to low and add shredded cheddar cheese to the milk mixture. Stir until the cheese is fully melted and the sauce is smooth.

5. **Season:**
   - Season the cheese sauce with salt and pepper to taste. Keep in mind that the cheese adds some saltiness, so start with a little and adjust as needed.

6. **Combine with Broccoli:**
   - Pour the cheese sauce over the steamed broccoli and gently toss to coat the broccoli with the cheesy goodness.

7. **Serve:**
   - Transfer the cheesy broccoli to a serving dish. It's now ready to be served as a delicious and comforting side dish.

## Tips for Little Chefs:

- Be cautious when handling hot items, and it's always a good idea to have a grown-up help.
- Encourage creativity by adding a sprinkle of Parmesan cheese, breadcrumbs, or a pinch of your favorite herbs to these dishes.

- Enjoy your tasty green beans and cheesy broccoli as a nutritious and flavorful addition to your meals!

## How you do you make homemade gravy?

Making homemade gravy is a simple and delicious way to enhance the flavors of your dishes. Here's a simplified recipe for homemade gravy:

# Ingredients:

- 2 tablespoons butter or pan drippings (from roasted meat)
- 2 tablespoons all-purpose flour
- 2 cups broth (chicken, beef, or vegetable)
- Salt and pepper to taste

# Instructions:

1. **Prepare the Roux:**
   - In a saucepan over medium heat, melt the butter or use pan drippings from a roasted meat.
2. **Add Flour:**
   - Sprinkle the flour over the melted butter or drippings. Whisk continuously to create a smooth paste, known as a roux.
3. **Cook the Roux:**

- Continue to cook the roux for 1-2 minutes, stirring constantly. This helps eliminate the raw flour taste.

4. **Gradually Add Broth:**
   - Gradually pour in the broth while whisking to avoid lumps. Keep whisking to ensure a smooth consistency.

5. **Simmer:**
   - Bring the mixture to a simmer over medium heat. Allow it to simmer until it reaches your desired thickness. If it becomes too thick, you can add more broth to achieve the consistency you prefer.

6. **Season:**
   - Season the gravy with salt and pepper to taste. You can also add any additional herbs or spices of your choice.

7. **Strain (Optional):**
   - If you want a smoother texture, you can strain the gravy to remove any lumps or bits. Use a fine mesh strainer or cheesecloth.

8. **Serve:**
   - Once the gravy has reached your desired thickness and flavor, it's ready to be served over mashed potatoes, roasted meats, or any dish of your choice.

## Tips for Little Chefs:

- Be careful when working with hot ingredients, and it's always a good idea to have a grown-up assist with the stove.
- You can customize the flavor of your gravy by adding herbs like thyme, rosemary, or a splash of Worcestershire sauce.
- Experiment with different broths to complement the dish you're serving the gravy with.

Making homemade gravy is a versatile skill that can elevate many meals. Enjoy your delicious homemade gravy!


## What are common cooking techniques and what do they mean?

Here are explanations of common cooking techniques along with examples, simplified for easy understanding:

# 1. Dredging:

- **Meaning:** Dredging involves coating food, typically meat or vegetables, with a dry ingredient like flour, breadcrumbs, or cornmeal before cooking.
- **Example:** Dredging chicken in flour before pan-frying to create a crispy and golden crust.

# 2. Roux:

- **Meaning:** A roux is a mixture of fat (usually butter) and flour used as a thickening agent in sauces and gravies.
- **Example:** Making a roux by melting butter, adding flour, and stirring until it forms a smooth paste before adding liquid to make a sauce.

## 3. Sear:

- **Meaning:** Searing is a technique where food, often meat, is cooked quickly at a high temperature to brown the exterior, creating a flavorful crust.
- **Example:** Searing a steak in a hot pan to achieve a caramelized outer layer while keeping the inside juicy.

## 4. Brown:

- **Meaning:** Browning involves cooking food over medium to high heat until it turns brown, enhancing its flavor through the Maillard reaction.
- **Example:** Browning onions in a pan before making soup, enhancing the overall flavor of the dish.

## 5. Saute:

- **Meaning:** Sautéing involves cooking food quickly over medium to high heat in a small amount of oil or fat.
- **Example:** Sautéing vegetables like bell peppers and mushrooms in a pan for a stir-fry.

## 6. Simmer:

- **Meaning:** Simmering is a gentle cooking technique where food is cooked in a liquid just below boiling, allowing flavors to meld without rapid boiling.
- **Example:** Simmering a stew on the stovetop to allow flavors to develop and meats to become tender.

## 7. Boil:

- **Meaning:** Boiling is cooking food in hot water at its boiling point (100°C or 212°F).
- **Example:** Boiling pasta in a pot of water until it becomes tender.

## 8. Grill:

- **Meaning:** Grilling involves cooking food over an open flame or heat source, often on a grate with visible grill marks.
- **Example:** Grilling burgers on a barbecue for a smoky flavor and distinctive grill marks.

## 9. Bake:

- **Meaning:** Baking is cooking food in an oven using dry heat, typically surrounding the food on all sides.
- **Example:** Baking cookies in the oven until they are golden brown and delicious.

## 10. Steam:

- **Meaning:** Steaming is cooking food by exposing it to steam, often over boiling water, retaining more nutrients compared to boiling.
- **Example:** Steaming vegetables like broccoli to preserve their color and nutrients.

These basic cooking techniques are the building blocks for many recipes, and understanding them allows for versatile and delicious cooking.

**How to easily make beautiful grill marks:**

Creating great grill marks on your food is not only visually appealing but can also add a delightful smoky flavor. Here's a simplified guide to achieving those perfect grill marks:

## Ingredients and Tools:

- Your choice of food for grilling (e.g., steaks, chicken, vegetables)
- Olive oil or marinade (optional)
- Salt and pepper for seasoning
- Preheated grill

## Instructions:

1. **Preheat the Grill:**
   - Ensure your grill is preheated to a medium-high to high heat. The grates should be hot before placing your food on them.
2. **Prepare the Food:**
   - Pat your food dry with paper towels to remove excess moisture, which can interfere with grill marks. If you're grilling meat, you can also brush it lightly with olive oil or your favorite marinade for added flavor.
3. **Season:**
   - Season your food with salt and pepper or your preferred seasonings.
4. **Place on the Grill at an Angle:**
   - Position the food on the preheated grill grates at a 45-degree angle to the bars. This initial angle allows for the first set of grill marks.
5. **Grill Without Disturbing:**

- Avoid moving or flipping the food too soon. Let it cook for a few minutes without disturbance to allow the grill marks to develop.

6. **Rotate for Crosshatch Marks:**
   - Once you have nice grill marks at the initial angle, rotate the food 90 degrees to create a crosshatch pattern. This will give you those classic diamond-shaped grill marks.

7. **Flip and Repeat:**
   - Carefully flip the food to the other side and repeat the process. Place the food at a 45-degree angle, allow it to cook, and then rotate for the crosshatch marks.

8. **Adjust Heat if Necessary:**
   - If you notice the grill marks are developing too quickly or not as desired, you can adjust the heat. Lower the heat slightly for a slower cooking process.

9. **Monitor Cooking Time:**
   - Keep an eye on the cooking time to ensure your food reaches the desired level of doneness. Cooking times will vary depending on the type and thickness of the food.

10. **Serve and Enjoy:**
    - Once your food is cooked to perfection with beautiful grill marks, remove it from

the grill and let it rest for a few minutes before serving.

## Tips:

- Clean and oil your grill grates regularly to prevent sticking and promote better grill marks.
- Use high-quality cuts of meat and fresh vegetables for optimal results.
- Experiment with different marinades and seasonings to enhance the flavor of your grilled dishes.

By following these steps, you can easily achieve those coveted grill marks, turning your grilled dishes into visually appealing and delicious masterpieces.

### How do you use a pressure cooker and what can you cook in it?

Using a pressure cooker can significantly speed up the cooking process and result in flavorful and tender dishes. Here's a simplified guide on how to use a pressure cooker and what you can cook in it:

## How to Use a Pressure Cooker:

1. **Ingredients:**
   - Gather the ingredients for your recipe. Pressure cookers work well with a variety of foods, including grains, beans, meat, and vegetables.
2. **Prep Ingredients:**
   - Chop, season, and prepare your ingredients as per your recipe.
3. **Add Ingredients to the Pot:**
   - Place the ingredients in the pressure cooker pot. Be mindful not to overfill it; leave some space for expansion.
4. **Add Liquid:**
   - Most pressure cooker recipes require liquid for the cooker to pressurize. This could be water, broth, or other liquids specified in your recipe.
5. **Secure the Lid:**
   - Make sure the pressure cooker lid is properly sealed and secure. Follow the manufacturer's instructions on how to lock the lid.
6. **Set Pressure and Time:**
   - Choose the pressure level (low or high) and set the cooking time using the control panel or dials on your pressure cooker.
7. **Start Cooking:**

- Turn on the pressure cooker and let it come to pressure. Once it reaches the desired pressure, the cooking time will begin.

8. **Natural or Quick Release:**
   - After the cooking time is complete, release the pressure. Some recipes may call for a natural release (letting the pressure drop on its own) or a quick release (manually releasing the pressure).

9. **Open the Lid Safely:**
   - Open the lid only when the pressure indicator shows that it's safe to do so. Be cautious of hot steam.

10. **Serve and Enjoy:**
   - Your dish is now ready to be served!

# What You Can Cook in a Pressure Cooker:

1. **Rice and Grains:**
   - Perfectly cook rice, quinoa, or other grains in a fraction of the time.

2. **Beans and Legumes:**
   - Speed up the cooking process for dried beans and lentils.

3. **Soups and Stews:**
   - Make hearty soups and stews with tender meats and vegetables.

4. **Chili:**

- Prepare flavorful chili in a short amount of time.

5. **Poultry:**
   - Cook chicken, turkey, or other poultry quickly for tender and juicy results.

6. **Beef and Pork:**
   - Tenderize tougher cuts of beef or pork for dishes like pot roast or pulled pork.

7. **Vegetables:**
   - Steam or cook vegetables for side dishes or incorporate them into main courses.

8. **Desserts:**
   - Some pressure cookers have features for making desserts like cheesecake or rice pudding.

9. **One-Pot Meals:**
   - Create one-pot wonders with a variety of ingredients for easy and quick meals.

10. **Broths and Stocks:**
    - Make rich and flavorful broths and stocks in a fraction of the time.

## Tips for Using a Pressure Cooker:

- Follow the manufacturer's instructions for your specific pressure cooker model.
- Ensure the pressure release valve is clear and functioning before each use.

- Experiment with cooking times and flavors to find what works best for your taste preferences.

Using a pressure cooker can be a game-changer in the kitchen, allowing you to prepare a wide range of dishes efficiently.

**What are the cuts of meat most commonly used?**

Several cuts of meat are commonly used in cooking, each offering unique flavors, textures, and best-suited cooking methods. Here are some popular cuts of meat:

# Beef:

1. **Chuck:**
    - Comes from the shoulder area; great for pot roasts and stews.
2. **Ribeye:**
    - A well-marbled cut from the rib section; known for its tenderness and rich flavor, often grilled or pan-seared.
3. **Filet Mignon:**
    - A tender and lean cut from the tenderloin; often used in upscale dishes.
4. **Sirloin:**
    - Cut from the hip area; versatile and can be grilled, roasted, or pan-fried.

5. **Brisket:**
   - A tough cut from the breast area; becomes tender and flavorful when slow-cooked.
6. **T-Bone and Porterhouse:**
   - Both cuts include a T-shaped bone with sections of strip steak and tenderloin; suitable for grilling.
7. **Flank Steak:**
   - A lean cut from the abdominal muscles; best when marinated and grilled or sliced thin for stir-fries.
8. **Ground Beef:**
   - Comes from various cuts; versatile and used in dishes like burgers, meatballs, and tacos.

# Pork:

1. **Pork Chop:**
   - Cut from the loin; can be boneless or bone-in and is suitable for grilling, baking, or pan-frying.
2. **Pork Tenderloin:**
   - A lean and tender cut; often roasted or grilled.
3. **Pork Shoulder (or Pork Butt):**
   - Ideal for slow-cooking, braising, or pulled pork recipes.
4. **Spareribs:**

- Cut from the belly and side; excellent for grilling or smoking.

5. **Bacon:**
    - Usually comes from pork belly; used for frying or baking.
6. **Ground Pork:**
    - Versatile and used in various dishes like meatballs, sausages, and stir-fries.

# Chicken:

1. **Breast:**
    - Lean and versatile; can be grilled, baked, sautéed, or used in various recipes.
2. **Thigh:**
    - Dark meat with more flavor; great for grilling, roasting, or braising.
3. **Drumstick:**
    - Dark meat with a bone; suitable for baking, frying, or grilling.
4. **Wings:**
    - Typically fried or baked and served with various sauces.
5. **Whole Chicken:**
    - Can be roasted whole or broken down into individual cuts for various cooking methods.

# Lamb:

1. **Lamb Chops:**
   - Cut from the loin or rib; can be grilled or pan-fried.
2. **Leg of Lamb:**
   - Often roasted whole or cut into chops.
3. **Shoulder:**
   - Suitable for slow-cooking, braising, or stewing.
4. **Shanks:**
   - Ideal for slow-cooking or braising.

# Veal:

1. **Veal Chop:**
   - Similar to pork or beef chops; can be grilled or pan-fried.
2. **Veal Scallopini:**
   - Thin slices ideal for sautéing.
3. **Osso Buco:**
   - Veal shanks often braised and served with a flavorful sauce.

These are general categories, and specific cuts may vary based on regional preferences and butchering methods. Each cut has its own characteristics, and the choice often depends on the desired outcome and cooking method.

**What is the difference between breadcrumbs and panko?**

Breadcrumbs and panko are both used as coatings in various recipes to add a crispy texture to fried or baked dishes, but they differ in terms of texture, ingredients, and origin.

# Breadcrumbs:

1. **Texture:**
   - Traditional breadcrumbs have a finer and softer texture compared to panko.
2. **Ingredients:**
   - Breadcrumbs are made from sliced or ground bread, often with the crust included. The bread may be fresh or slightly dried before processing.
3. **Production:**
   - The bread is typically processed into crumbs using a food processor, blender, or by hand. Breadcrumbs can be plain or seasoned, depending on the recipe.
4. **Absorption:**
   - Breadcrumbs may absorb less oil during frying compared to panko due to their finer texture.
5. **Common Uses:**

- Used as a coating for various dishes such as breaded chicken, fish, or vegetables. Also used as a binder in meatballs and meatloaf.

## Panko:

1. **Texture:**
   - Panko has a coarser, flakier texture compared to traditional breadcrumbs. The flakes are larger and irregularly shaped.
2. **Ingredients:**
   - Panko is made from bread without crusts, resulting in a lighter and airier texture. The bread used is often specially prepared with an electric current to create larger, flakier crumbs.
3. **Production:**
   - Panko is made through a unique process that involves baking bread with an electric current, resulting in a crustless loaf. The loaf is then processed into large, airy crumbs.
4. **Absorption:**
   - Panko tends to absorb less oil during frying, making it popular for creating a light and crispy texture.
5. **Common Uses:**
   - Widely used in Japanese cuisine, panko is often employed as a coating for tempura

and other fried dishes. It has become popular in Western cooking for its ability to create a crispier crust.

## Summary:

- **Texture:** Breadcrumbs have a finer texture, while panko has a coarser and flakier texture.
- **Ingredients:** Breadcrumbs are made from sliced or ground bread, while panko is made from crustless bread, resulting in a lighter texture.
- **Absorption:** Panko tends to absorb less oil during frying, contributing to a lighter and crispier coating.
- **Common Uses:** Both are used as coatings, but panko is often preferred when a lighter and crunchier texture is desired, especially in recipes like fried seafood or vegetables.

Choosing between breadcrumbs and panko depends on the desired outcome of the dish. Panko is particularly popular when a light and crispy texture is crucial, while traditional breadcrumbs may be preferred for certain recipes that benefit from a finer texture.

1. **Little Chef Basics:**
   - We covered handwashing, food danger zone awareness, and the importance of proper temperature measurement and knife safety for Little Chefs.
2. **Kitchen Skills:**
   - Explored knife skills, peeling vegetables, and essential utensils for Little Chefs.
3. **Measuring Ingredients:**
   - Discussed how to measure dry and wet ingredients accurately.
4. **Simple Snacks:**
   - Explored easy snacks and 10 yummy parfaits for Little Chefs.
5. **Recipes:**
   - Covered recipes for peanut butter and banana rolls, along with an overview of foodborne illnesses and cross-contamination.
6. **Crockpot Cooking:**
   - Provided 20 simple crockpot meals and recipes, followed by 10 more, and another set of 10, including tips for preparation.
7. **Pasta Cooking:**
   - Explained how to boil pasta, test its doneness, and the meaning of "al dente."

8. **Meatballs and More:**
   - Covered cooking frozen meatballs for spaghetti, making meatball subs, barbecue little smokies or meatballs, and creating pigs in a blanket.
9. **Frying and Casseroles:**
   - Explored frying breaded pork chops and provided 10 casserole recipes with exact instructions.
10. **Pizza and Chicken Dumplings:**
    - Shared a simplified homemade pizza recipe and explained how to make chicken and dumplings.
11. **Unique Recipes:**
    - Explored the concept of a pizza burger and provided a recipe.
12. **Vegetables:**
    - Explored recipes for tasty green beans and cheesy broccoli, along with the importance of eating more veggies.
13. **Homemade Gravy:**
    - Provided a simplified recipe for making homemade gravy.
14. **Common Cooking Techniques:**
    - Explained common cooking techniques like dredging, roux, searing, and browning.
15. **Grill Marks:**
    - Shared tips on creating great grill marks made easy.

16. **Pressure Cooker:**
    - Explained how to use a pressure cooker and listed dishes suitable for pressure cooking.
17. **Meat Cuts:**
    - Discussed common cuts of meat for beef, pork, chicken, lamb, and veal.
18. **Breadcrumbs vs. Panko:**
    - Differentiated between breadcrumbs and panko in terms of texture, ingredients, and common uses.
19. **Summary:**
    - Explored a variety of cooking topics and skills, focusing on simplicity and safety for Little Chefs.

## Summary:

In this book, we covered a range of topics for aspiring little chefs. We started with kitchen basics like handwashing, safety, and temperature awareness. We discussed essential skills like knife use, utensil knowledge, and proper ingredient measurement. Simple snacks and 10 yummy parfaits were introduced, followed by recipes for peanut butter and banana rolls. We explored food safety, crockpot meals, pasta cooking, and meatball recipes.

The discussion expanded to frying techniques, casseroles, pizza, and unique recipes like pizza burgers. Vegetables took the spotlight with recipes for green beans and cheesy broccoli, emphasizing their importance. A simplified homemade gravy recipe was shared. We delved into common cooking techniques, grill marks, and the versatility of a pressure cooker with suitable dishes.

Conclusion:

This book also covered various meat cuts for beef, pork, chicken, lamb, and veal. The difference between breadcrumbs and panko was explained. The summary emphasizes a diverse range of cooking skills, recipes, and safety measures tailored for young chefs.

In conclusion, this book is aimed to provide a comprehensive and simplified guide for aspiring young chefs. We covered essential kitchen skills, safety practices, and a variety of recipes ranging from simple snacks to more advanced dishes. The focus was on fostering a love for cooking while emphasizing the importance of hygiene, proper techniques, and understanding ingredients.

We explored a wide array of topics, including pasta cooking, crockpot meals, frying, baking, and using a pressure cooker. Additionally, we discussed the nuances of different cuts of meat, the distinctions between breadcrumbs and panko, and the significance of incorporating vegetables into meals.

Overall, the book aimed to inspire curiosity and creativity in the kitchen, encouraging young chefs to explore diverse recipes and cooking techniques while always prioritizing safety and hygiene. The journey from basic skills to more complex recipes was tailored to make the culinary world accessible and enjoyable for budding cooks.